21st Century Skills Library

REAL WORLD MATH: NATURAL DISASTERS

EARTHQUAKES

BY GRAEME DAVIS

CHERRY LAKE
Publishing

Published in the United States of America by
Cherry Lake Publishing, Ann Arbor, Michigan
www.cherrylakepublishing.com

Content Adviser
Jack Williams
Founding editor of the *USA Today* weather page and author of *The AMS Weather Book: The Ultimate Guide to America's Weather*

Math Adviser
Katherine M. Gregory, M.Ed

Credits
Cover and page 1, ©Nigelspiers/Dreamstime.com; page 4, ©iBird/Shutterstock, Inc.; page 8, ©iStockphoto.com/Proioxis; page 12, ©Hupeng/Dreamstime.com; page 14, ©Silverkblack/Shutterstock, Inc.; page 17, ©David Gysel/Alamy; page 18, ©North Wind Picture Archives via AP Images; page 20, ©olling/Shutterstock, Inc.; page 23, ©Lowe Llaguno/Shutterstock, Inc.; page 24, ©Javarman/Dreamstime.com; page 26, ©iStockphoto.com/Lokibaho; page 28, ©akiyoko/Shutterstock, Inc.

Library of Congress Cataloging-in-Publication Data
Davis, Graeme, 1958–
 Earthquakes / by Graeme Davis.
     p. cm.—(Real world math)
 Includes bibliographical references and index.
 ISBN 978-1-61080-323-6 (lib. bdg.)—ISBN 978-1-61080-332-8 (e-book)—
ISBN 978-1-61080-411-0 (pbk.)
 1. Earthquakes—Juvenile literature. 2. Mathematics—Juvenile literature.
I. Title. II. Series.
 QE521.3.D38 2012
 551.22—dc23   2011032619

Cherry Lake Publishing would like to acknowledge
the work of The Partnership for 21st Century Skills.
Please visit *www.21stcenturyskills.org* for more information.

Printed in the United States of America
Corporate Graphics Inc.
January 2012
CLSP10

TABLE OF CONTENTS

CHAPTER ONE
WHEN THE EARTH SHAKES

Imagine you are at home, eating dinner. Suddenly, you feel a bump, as though someone walked into the table. The plates in the cabinet rattle. The house begins to shake.

Earthquakes can cause major damage to homes, businesses, and other buildings.

A picture falls off the wall and crashes to the floor. You quickly realize that the ground beneath you is moving. You're experiencing an earthquake!

Most earthquakes are caused by the movement of the earth's **tectonic plates**. Earth's rocky outer layer is made up of about one dozen large plates and several smaller ones. The area where two plates meet is called a **geological fault**. The plates bumping into one another at a fault is what causes earthquakes.

Most of the time, the ground on either side of a fault is still. When enough pressure builds up to overcome **friction**, the ground moves and **shock waves** spread out like ripples on a pond. Those shock waves are what most people think of when they think of earthquakes.

21ST CENTURY CONTENT

Scientists at the U.S. Geological Survey (USGS) keep an eye on earthquakes, volcanoes, landslides, and other natural disasters around the world. The USGS's staff includes 10,000 scientists, technicians, and support personnel who work at more than 400 locations throughout the United States. The organization also provides scientific support and information to more than 100 countries around the world.

Shock waves can travel through the ground very quickly, reaching speeds of up to 5 miles (8 kilometers) per second. That's 24 times the speed of sound. The ground shakes and tears apart, and buildings can be damaged or destroyed. Earthquakes at sea can cause **tsunamis**, huge waves that race across the ocean at 400 to 500 miles (643 to 805 km) per hour. Tsunamis can cause terrible damage when they reach land.

There are two main types of earthquake **vibrations**. P waves shake the ground from side to side. S waves make the ground move up and down. P waves travel faster than S waves, so they are usually felt first. Using S and P waves, geologists can determine the distance to an earthquake's **epicenter**. The epicenter is the area on the earth's surface directly above where an earthquake strikes. Geologists measure the time between P waves and S waves on a **seismograph**. Seismographs are set up at earthquake recording stations. When three or more seismographs have recorded the earthquake, scientists find the epicenter by using a mathematical technique called **triangulation**.

Scientists use scales of **magnitude**, or strength, to report the power of an earthquake. The Richter scale is the one most commonly used. It rates the power of an earthquake from 0 to 10, with 10 being the most powerful. The biggest earthquake in recorded history was magnitude 9.5. It struck

Chile in 1960. The biggest earthquake in U.S. history was magnitude 9.2 and struck Alaska in 1964. Any earthquake of magnitude 5.0 or higher can cause damage to buildings. Magnitude 3.0–4.0 earthquakes cause little or no damage. Earthquakes of magnitude 2.0 or less are usually too small to feel.

REAL WORLD MATH CHALLENGE

Scientists use two different kinds of vibrations, called P waves and S waves, to calculate the distance between a recording station and the epicenter of an earthquake. P waves travel more quickly than S waves. The distance to the epicenter in kilometers is roughly equal to 8 times the interval (in seconds) between the first P wave and the first S wave reaching the station.

If the first S wave arrives 37 seconds after the first P wave, how many kilometers away is the epicenter? How many miles does that equal?

(1 kilometer = 0.62 miles)

(Turn to page 29 for the answers)

CHAPTER TWO
EARTH'S PLATES IN MOTION

Tectonic plates move very slowly. Earthquakes can be caused when two plates bump into one another or slide and grind past one other. Volcanoes can also form at that point, as

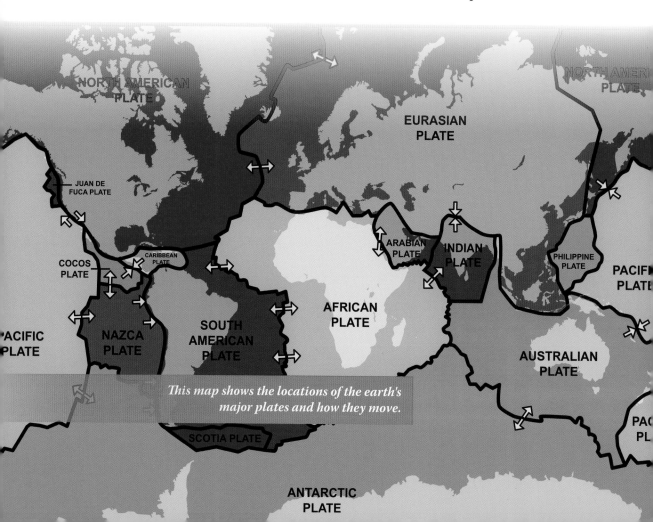

This map shows the locations of the earth's major plates and how they move.

NORTH AMERICAN PLATE

EURASIAN PLATE

NORTH AMERICAN PLATE

JUAN DE FUCA PLATE

ARABIAN PLATE

INDIAN PLATE

PHILIPPINE PLATE

PACIFIC PLATE

COCOS PLATE

CARIBBEAN PLATE

PACIFIC PLATE

NAZCA PLATE

SOUTH AMERICAN PLATE

AFRICAN PLATE

AUSTRALIAN PLATE

SCOTIA PLATE

PACIFIC PLATE

ANTARCTIC PLATE

magma from the inner portions of the earth rises up into the gaps between the two plates.

The Pacific Plate is the largest of the tectonic plates. Its eastern, northern, and western edges are sometimes called the Ring of Fire. The Ring of Fire is shaped like an upside-down *U*. It runs from New Zealand through Indonesia, the Philippines, and Japan, then across to Alaska and down the Pacific coasts of Canada and the United States. About 90 percent of the world's earthquakes take place along the Ring of Fire. Many volcanoes also erupt in this area.

Two smaller plates, the Cocos and Nazca Plates, lie between the Pacific Plate and the South American Plate. The Ring of Fire continues along the eastern edges of these plates, from Mexico to Chile.

The Australian-Indian Plate and the African Plate push against the Eurasian Plate. This movement has lifted up the Himalayas, the Alps, and other mountain ranges in the region. It has caused earthquakes from Spain to Malaysia.

The African Plate is slowly pulling away from the Arabian Plate. This is causing earthquakes along the Red Sea and down Africa's Great Rift Valley.

The movement of tectonic plates is actually making the Atlantic Ocean bigger. The North American and South American Plates are pulling away from the Eurasian and African Plates. Magma from the earth's interior rises up to fill

LIFE & CAREER SKILLS

Whenever there is a serious earthquake, people need help. Have you ever asked yourself what you can do to help?

There are many international charities that send relief workers and supplies to areas affected by earthquakes and other natural disasters. They include the International Red Cross, Save the Children, the United Nations Children's Fund (UNICEF), Doctors Without Borders, and the International Fund for Animal Welfare. Often these charities and others like them accept donations to help the victims of a particular disaster.

Some people organize collections at their school or workplace. Others set up donation jars in local stores. When a disaster strikes, some charities publish lists of materials they need, such as clothing, blankets, medical supplies, bottled water, and canned foods. The organizations set up collection points where you can drop off the items you want to donate.

the gap, creating the Mid-Atlantic Spreading Ridge. Iceland is the only place where this ridge is above water. Iceland is growing wider by about 0.75 inches (2 centimeters) every year.

The Caribbean Plate is one of the smallest plates. Where it moves against the plates around it, however, it causes earthquakes that affect Mexico, Colombia, Venezuela, and other Caribbean nations.

REAL WORLD MATH CHALLENGE

This chart lists the biggest earthquakes in 2010. What fraction of the total number of earthquakes occurred along the Ring of Fire? Convert this fraction to a decimal.

Date	Location	Magnitude	Ring of Fire?
February 27	Offshore Bio-Bio, Chile	8.8	Yes
July 23	Moro Gulf, Mindanao, Philippines	7.6	Yes
July 23	Moro Gulf, Mindanao, Philippines	7.4	Yes
July 23	Moro Gulf, Mindanao, Philippines	7.3	Yes
April 4	Baja California, Mexico	7.2	Yes
May 9	Northern Sumatra, Indonesia	7.2	Yes
January 3	Solomon Islands	7.1	Yes
January 12	Haiti region	7.0	No
September 3	South Island of New Zealand	7.0	Yes
April 13	Southern Qinghai, China	6.9	No
January 10	Offshore Northern California	6.5	Yes
March 8	Eastern Turkey	6.1	No

(Turn to page 29 for the answer)

CHAPTER THREE

DO THE MATH: THE JAPANESE EARTHQUAKE OF 2011

About 80 miles (129 km) off the east coast of Japan, the huge Pacific Plate pushes against the tiny Okhotsk Plate. At 2:46 p.m. on March 11, 2011, a piece of the Pacific

Thousands of people were left homeless after the 2011 earthquake in Japan.

Plate 190 miles (306 km) wide pushed under the Okhotsk. The Okhotsk moved about 65 feet (20 meters). This happened about 15 miles (24 km) deep within the earth's crust. The vibrations produced by this action caused one of the five biggest earthquakes ever recorded.

The 2011 Tōhoku earthquake, named for the region of Japan nearest the quake, registered magnitude 9.0 on the Richter scale. It caused tsunami waves up to 33 feet (10 m) high, which washed inland as far as 6 miles (9.7 km). More than 125,000 buildings were destroyed or damaged, including three nuclear reactors at a huge power plant. The Japanese government ordered hundreds of thousands of people to **evacuate** the area in case there was a nuclear accident.

The earthquake damaged roads and railroads over a wide area. Millions of people were left without power or water. A dam collapsed, releasing water that washed away 1,800 houses. The tsunami tossed cars, trains, and buildings around like toys. Ships and boats were violently swept up onto the shorelines.

As the people of Japan began the challenging task of cleaning up, scientists explained that the damage could have been much worse. Collapsing buildings and fires cause most of the deaths and injuries in an earthquake. But Japan has very strict building codes to keep earthquake damage to a minimum. Japan's tough laws saved thousands of lives.

In the days after the earthquake, the region suffered hundreds of **aftershocks**. Some of them were magnitude 7.0, making them serious earthquakes. The biggest worry, though, was the three damaged nuclear reactors. More than three months after the earthquake, workers were still trying to make the damaged reactors safe. Some 85,000 people still could not return to their homes near the power plant.

Many acres of farmland were ruined by saltwater. It may be years before good crops can be grown on that land.

Nuclear meltdowns were a major concern after the 2011 Tohoku earthquake.

Thousands of fishing boats were damaged, a serious blow to Japan's important fishing industry. Because Japan is a powerful industrial nation, the damage there affected stock markets around the world. The earthquake may end up costing the world more than $200 billion.

LEARNING & INNOVATION SKILLS

Japan's National Police Agency puts the death toll from the 2011 earthquake at more than 15,000 people. In the year 869, an earthquake in the same area killed an estimated 1,000 people. The earthquake of 869 was estimated at magnitude 8.6, making it slightly less powerful than the magnitude 9.0 quake of 2011. Do you think this is the only reason why casualties were so much higher in 2011? What other reasons can you think of for the higher casualty figures of the more recent quake?

21ST CENTURY SKILLS LIBRARY

REAL WORLD MATH CHALLENGE

The following chart lists earthquakes of magnitude 9.0 or higher that occurred between 1912 and 2011. Calculate how many years passed between each earthquake. Put your answers in the "Interval" column. What are the shortest and longest intervals?

Year	Location	Interval (in years)	Magnitude
1952	Siberia	?	9.0
1960	Chile	?	9.5
1964	Alaska	?	9.2
2004	Indonesia	?	9.1
2011	Japan	?	9.0

(Turn to page 29 for the answers)

Earthquakes with higher magnitudes stand a greater chance of causing serious damage.

CHAPTER FOUR

DO THE MATH: THE NEXT BIG ONE?

If you live in California, you might have heard people talking about "the next big one." California sits on the San Andreas Fault, where the Pacific Plate slides along the

Many people were injured or killed during the San Francisco earthquake of 1906.

North American Plate. Every day, dozens of earthquakes are recorded in California, although most of them are too small to feel. But there have been deadly earthquakes in California. Scientists think that it's only a matter of time before "the next big one" strikes.

Between 1906 and 2006, California suffered 63 earthquakes of magnitude 5.0 or greater, and countless smaller ones. The deadliest earthquake in California history was the San Francisco earthquake of 1906. The U.S. Geological Survey estimates that more than 3,000 people died in this magnitude 7.8 quake, the second largest in California's history. Fires caused by broken gas pipes destroyed about 25,000 buildings.

LEARNING & INNOVATION SKILLS

California is home to more than 37 million people, which is more than 12 percent of the total U.S. population. It also suffers more earthquakes than any other U.S. state. Why do you think so many people want to live in California despite the risk of earthquakes? If you live in California, what are the great things about your home state that keep you living there? If you live somewhere else, what are the things about California that would make you want to move there?

Up to three-quarters of the city's population were left homeless.

In 1994, a magnitude 6.7 earthquake struck the Los Angeles area, near the town of Northridge. Around 60 people were killed and more than 7,000 injured, mostly as a result of buildings falling down. Elevated highways collapsed in a few places. Fires and landslides added to the damage.

Collapsed highways can be a major hassle to drivers.

REAL WORLD MATH CHALLENGE

The table below shows the number of earthquakes recorded in a single day in 2011.

What was the total number of earthquakes recorded? Which state had the most earthquakes? Which state (or states) experienced earthquakes of the highest magnitude?

State	Magnitude			Total Number of Quakes
	1.0–1.9	2.0–2.9	3.0–3.9	
California	38	9	1	48
Alaska	14	6	3	23
Arizona	1			1
Utah	2			2
Arkansas	2	1		3
Washington	2			2
Hawaii	3			3
Montana	1			1
Oregon	2			2
Nevada	2			2
Texas			1	1
Missouri	1			1

[Turn to page 29 for the answers]

The California Emergency Management Agency works with local government and businesses to ensure that Californians are as well prepared for a quake as possible. California building codes require new buildings to be earthquake-resistant. Practice earthquake drills are held regularly so people know what to do when one strikes.

California is not the only earthquake danger zone in the United States. The Pacific Northwest states of Oregon and Washington lie along the dangerous Cascadia fault line that runs from Northern California into Canadian waters. Some experts believe that the area is overdue for a massive quake. Major quakes have also struck Alaska, including a magnitude 9.2 that hit in 1964. At that time, it was the second-largest earthquake in recorded history.

The East Coast of the United States also faces the threat of earthquakes. Although there's less activity than in California or the Pacific Northwest, a smaller quake could cause massive destruction. Building codes in the East are less strict. Heavily populated cities such as New York, Boston, Philadelphia, and Washington, D.C., could suffer terribly if a quake struck.

Earthquakes are almost impossible to predict. No one knows when or where "the next big one" will strike. The only certainty is that it will happen.

Buildings in California are built carefully to protect against future earthquake damage.

CHAPTER FIVE
SURVIVAL!

There are many dangers in an earthquake. Buildings can fall down, or pieces of them can fall off and injure people. Damaged gas lines can cause raging fires. Rocks can shake loose from cliffs and mountains. The ground can soften and

Signs warn people of areas where falling rocks are common.

flow like water, causing deadly landslides. What can we do to make earthquakes less dangerous?

Buildings can be made earthquake-resistant in many ways. Some buildings are mounted on shock absorbers. Taller buildings sometimes have moving weights inside that counteract the force of an earthquake. Modern buildings can be constructed with tougher, more flexible building materials that can "give" with the rumblings of an earthquake.

The inside of a building can be made safer by making sure that tall, heavy pieces of furniture cannot fall over. Bookshelves and other large pieces can be bolted into the walls or floors so that they will not topple in an earthquake.

LIFE & CAREER SKILLS

If you live in an earthquake zone, your school probably has regular earthquake drills. What are the most important things to remember when an earthquake hits? Do you need to do anything different if you are at home, at the mall, or outdoors?

The Federal Emergency Management Agency has developed a three-part personal safety plan in the event of an earthquake: Drop, Cover, and Hold On. When you feel an earthquake, drop to the ground. Take cover under a sturdy table or other piece of furniture. Then hold on until the shaking stops. If there's no table near you, cover your face and head with your arms and crouch in an inside corner of the

Tables and desks are good sources of shelter during earthquakes.

building. Stay away from windows, outside doors, walls, and anything that could fall, such as lighting fixtures and tall furniture.

After an earthquake, there is a danger that gas lines and gas tanks may be damaged. Use your nose and ears to smell and listen for escaping gas. If you smell or hear gas, go outside immediately.

An earthquake's unstoppable fury is a reminder of the powerful forces at work on our shifting, constantly changing planet. There is nothing we can do to prevent an earthquake from happening. But by preparing for a quake, we can learn to protect ourselves and reduce the chance of getting injured.

REAL WORLD MATH CHALLENGE

Damage from a 1933 earthquake in Long Beach, California, cost $40 million. The 1994 Northridge earthquake cost $20 billion. One dollar in 1933 is worth $16.73 today. One dollar in 1994 is worth $1.50 today. What is the cost of each earthquake in today's money?

(Turn to page 29 for the answers)

Earthquakes can easily move heavy objects such as cars and trucks.

REAL WORLD MATH CHALLENGE ANSWERS

Chapter One

Page 7

The epicenter is 296 kilometers away.

$37 \times 8 = 296$

296 kilometers is equal to 183.52 miles.

$296 \times 0.62 = 183.52$

Chapter Two

Page 11

3/4 of the earthquakes listed occurred along the Ring of Fire.

9 earthquakes out of 12, or 9/12, reduced to 3/4

3/4 is equal to 0.75.

$3 \div 4 = 0.75$

Chapter Three

Page 16

Year	Location	Interval (in years)	Magnitude
1952	Siberia	-	9.0
1960	Chile	8	9.5
1964	Alaska	4	9.2
2004	Indonesia	40	9.1
2011	Japan	7	9.0

$1960 - 1952 = 8$ years

$1964 - 1960 = 4$ years

$2004 - 1964 = 40$ years

$2011 - 2004 = 7$ years

The longest interval is 40 years.

The shortest interval is 4 years.

Chapter Four

Page 21

A total of 89 earthquakes were recorded on this day.

$48 + 23 + 1 + 2 + 3 + 2 + 3 + 1 + 2 + 2 + 1 + 1 = 89$ total earthquakes

California had the most earthquakes (48).

California, Alaska, and Texas all had magnitude 3.0–3.9 earthquakes, making them the most severe.

Chapter Five

Page 27

The 1933 Long Beach earthquake cost $669.2 million.

$40,000,000 \times $16.73 = $669,200,000

The 1971 Northridge earthquake cost $103 billion.

$20,000,000,000 \times $1.50 = $30,000,000,000

GLOSSARY

aftershocks (AF-tuhr-shawks) smaller earthquakes that take place after a large one

epicenter (EH-pih-sen-tur) the area on the earth's surface directly above the place where an earthquake strikes

evacuate (i-VAK-yoo-wate) to move out of danger

friction (FRIK-shuhn) rubbing; the force that slows down objects when they rub against each other

geological fault (jee-uh-LAW-juh-kul FAWLT) a tear in the earth where two tectonic plates meet

magma (MAG-muh) melted rock found beneath the earth's surface

magnitude (MAG-nuh-tood) the measured power of an earthquake

seismograph (SIZE-muh-graf) an instrument that detects earthquakes and measures their power

shock waves (SHAWK WAYVZ) ripples that spread out from an earthquake, an explosion, or some other violent event

tectonic plates (tek-TON-ik PLATES) huge, thick landmasses that make up Earth's outer layer they drift atop softer material that lies beneath them

triangulation (tryan-gyuh-LAY-shun) a method used to calculate the position of something using distances and angles from two or more other locations

tsunamis (tsoo-NAH-meez) large, fast-moving waves caused by an underwater earthquake or volcano

vibrations (vye-BRAY-shuhnz) shaking motions

FOR MORE INFORMATION

BOOKS

Benoit, Peter. *The Haitian Earthquake of 2010*. New York: Scholastic, 2011.

Green, Jen. *Surviving Natural Disasters*. London: Arcturus Publishing, 2010.

Griffey, Harriet. *Earthquakes and Other Natural Disasters*. New York: Dorling Kindersley, 2010.

Markovics, Joyce. *Saving Animals After Earthquakes*. New York: Bearport Publishing, 2011.

WEB SITES

BBC News—Animated Guide: Earthquakes
http://news.bbc.co.uk/2/hi/science/nature/7533950.stm
Have fun looking at a colorful animation that shows how, where, and why earthquakes and other natural disasters occur.

The Great California ShakeOut
www.shakeout.org
This site offers helpful, life-saving information on how to prepare for earthquakes.

U.S. Geological Survey: Earthquakes for Kids
http://earthquake.usgs.gov/learn/kids/
Check out this site for earthquake facts, animations, pictures, and science fair projects.

INDEX

ABOUT THE AUTHOR

Graeme Davis was born in England and now lives in Virginia, where he experienced the magnitude 5.8 earthquake of August 2011. He's glad it was a small one! He has written more than 70 books and also works in the video games industry, where he uses his math skills every day.